HARVEST FESTIVALS AROUND THE WORLD

WRITTEN AND ILLUSTRATED BY
JUDITH HOFFMAN CORWIN

D0101287

JULIAN Ⓜ MESSNER
PUBLISHED BY SILVER BURDETT PRESS
PARSIPPANY, NEW JERSEY

Copyright ©1995 by Judith Hoffman Corwin

All rights reserved including the right of
reproduction in whole or in part in any form.
Published by Julian Messner, a division of
Silver Burdett Press, 299 Jefferson Road, Parsippany, New Jersey 07054.

JULIAN MESSNER and colophon are trademarks of Simon and Schuster

Book design by Anahid Hamparian

For Jules Arthur and Oliver Jamie

10 9 8 7 6 5 4 3 2 1

Library of Congress Cataloging-in-Publication Data

Corwin, Judith Hoffman.
    Harvest festivals around the world / Judith Hoffman Corwin.
1. Harvest Festivals--Juvenile literature. (1. Harvest festivals.)
I. Title.
GT4380.C67 1995
394.2'64--dc20

ISBN 0-671-87239-7 (hardcover)
ISBN 0-671-87240-0 (paperback)

95-32134
CIP
AC

CONTENTS

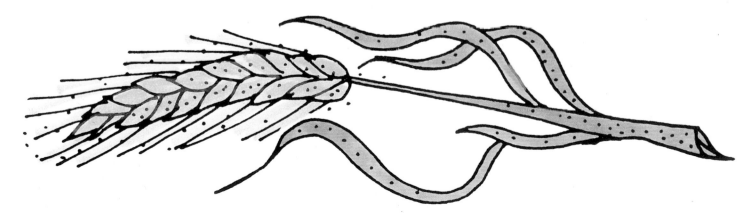

INTRODUCTION

AUTUMN — the season of reward — is harvest time. After the summer sun has completed its task, people gather in the fields, orchards, vineyards, and gardens to celebrate their hard work. During harvest time, grains, fruits, and vegetables are gathered and stored for the rest of the year. The seeds planted in the spring have been carefully watched, watered, and weeded until it is time to harvest. Experience as well as instinct tell people when the moment is right.

Everyone is involved in harvesting the crops. Work continues all day and sometimes into the night as harvesters rush to gather the crop before it spoils or the rain comes. At the end of the harvest, people are exhausted and look forward to a celebration. And that's when the festivals are held.

Harvest festivals are as numerous as the crops produced and the regions in which they grow. There are festivals for corn, onion, pumpkin, yam, melon, grape, hop, rice, barley, wheat, sugar cane, and apple. In all parts of the world, farmers gather to sing, dance, feast, and toast the end of the growing cycle.

EARLY HARVEST FESTIVALS

In ancient times, the gathering of the harvest was often celebrated with religious rituals. People usually offered the first part of the harvest to the gods as thanks and as a way of winning future favor. The corn mother was a common figure at harvest time. Usually made from the last or best sheaf cut of corn, her image was carried proudly from the field.

In ancient Israel, the harvest festival of Succoth was celebrated with a feast. The ancient Egyptians had more than one harvest. One of their festivals honored Min, the god they believed made the earth fertile, or rich. In the New World, Native Americans celebrated the harvest long before people from Europe arrived. In our May, which is autumn in South America, the ancient Incas held a festival called the Song of the Harvest. They offered the first corn to their gods.

HARVEST FESTIVALS TODAY

Today, in the United States, people celebrate an autumn ritual—the feast of Thanksgiving. All across the country in cities, towns, and rural areas; rich and poor; young and old; gather to offer thanks for what they have received. The spirit of Thanksgiving is common to all harvest festivals in all cultures. Prayers are expressed for a good year, good health, and prosperity.

The cultures and celebrations described in *Harvest Festivals Around the World* are accompanied by a project that is simple and fun to do. Each project will help to bring a culture to life. You may wish to work on the project alone, or with a friend or family member. Whatever you choose, the goal is to have fun and to experience the flavor of another land. Enjoy!

HARVEST SYMBOLS

THESE SIMPLE, BOLD DESIGNS symbolize the harvest from ancient times to the present day. How many do you recognize?

The symbols can be copied from this book. Just copy the pattern with tracing paper. Begin by placing a piece of tracing paper over the pattern shown here. Using a soft lead pencil, copy the outline. Turn the paper over and rub all over the pattern with your pencil. Turn it over again and tape or hold it down carefully on the paper or fabric you have chosen to work with. Draw over your original lines, pressing hard on the pencil. Lift the tracing paper pattern and you are ready to go.

Harvest Moon-This is a full moon, the second full moon in a specific month. It usually has a pinkish, yellow glow and appears even larger than the regular full moon. The harvest moon was important to farmers because it gave them an extra night's worth of light in which to bring in their crops.

Inca Sun God-He was the most powerful of all the gods worshipped by the ancient Incas. The sun with its warmth and brightness reminded the Incas of gold, a highly prized treasure of their empire.

Cornucopia-Since ancient times this has been the symbol of the harvest and good crops. The shape itself has its roots in ancient Greek folklore and recalls the practice of decorating a goat's horns with flowers, fruits, and corn. Thus dressed, the goat would never want for anything. Even today, the twisted horn has developed into a symbol of abundance. It is also called a horn of plenty.

Sunflower-These are the largest flowers on earth. Their heads can be 12 inches across and they can grow between 6 and 9 feet high! They love the sun and face it to grow tall. Sunflower petals are yellow like the sun and the center cluster of seeds are brown like the earth.

HARVEST BREAD

BREAD — WHAT A delicious taste treat! Almost every culture has its own kind. There is crusty Italian bread, Indian flat bread, Russian dark bread, Swedish braided bread, or Chinese steamed bread. Bread comes in many sizes and shapes — round, square, large, small, long, narrow, braided, twisted. It can be soft or hard, moist or dry, light or dark. The variety is amazing.

Most common forms of bread come from grain such as corn, barley, millet, buckwheat, and oats. These grains are planted, looked after, and eventually harvested. The harvested grain is ground by a mill or crushed into flour. The flour is then added to other ingredients and either baked, boiled, fried, or steamed. The result is delicious bread.

Scientists have traced bread as one of the oldest foods. They have evidence of a crude form dating from 12,000 years ago! It was made out of ground nuts, roots, and other fibers. Bread is so important that people have fought wars over it. Bread has been used for money, barter, decoration, and magic. Religions use bread in their ceremonies.

Some of the first breads were flat breads, baked in ancient Egypt. Until the last 200 years, white bread made from finely ground grain, was a luxury that only the wealthy or nobles could afford. The peasants had to be content with eating coarse, dark breads made from rye, barley, or oats. Today coarse, dark breads are regarded as having greater nutritional value, while white loaves are seen as having little nutritional value.

A BASIC BREAD RECIPE

Would you like to bake your very own loaf of bread? Why not give it a try? Here's a simple recipe for a delicious loaf. You may want to make two, one for yourself and one for a friend or relatives.

INGREDIENTS

- *2 packages active dry yeast*
- *3/4 cup of lukewarm water*
- *1 1/4 cups milk*
- *5 cups all purpose flour*
- *1/4 cup sweet butter, softened*
- *2 tablespoons sugar*
- *2 teaspoons baking powder*
- *2 teaspoons salt*
- *extra flour to knead the dough*
- *vegetable oil to grease the loaf pan*
- *3 tablespoons sweet butter, softened*

WHAT YOU WILL NEED

- *measuring cups and spoons*
- *large mixing bowl, mixing spoon*
- *9x5x3 inch metal loaf pan*
- *clean dish cloth*
- *rolling pin*
- *pot holders*

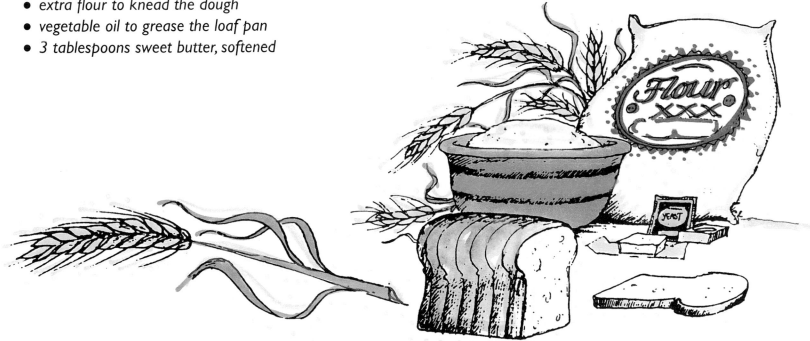

HOW TO DO IT

1. Before you begin, be sure to wash your hands and ask an adult to help you to use the oven.
2. Put the water in the mixing bowl and add the yeast. Stir until the yeast is dissolved.
3. Add the milk, 2 1/2 cups of flour, 1/4 cup of butter, sugar, baking powder, and salt. Mix.
4. Stir in the remaining flour and keep mixing the dough until it is soft and slightly sticky.
5. Knead the dough. First, spread out some of the extra flour on a clean kitchen counter and onto your hands. Press the palms of your hands into the dough, turning it around as you are working. This mixes the dough and distributes the air bubbles evenly through the dough. Knead the dough for about 5 minutes, until it is elastic and not sticky. Place in pan.
6. Spread 2 tablespoons of softened butter across the top of the dough and cover it with the clean dish cloth. Put this in a warm place and let it rise until it is doubled in size, about 1 hour. The dough will rise at least 2" above the pan in the center.
7. Preheat the over to 425degrees. Bake for 30 to 35 minutes or until the loaf is golden brown on top. Spread another tablespoon of soft butter on the top of the bread and allow to cool before slicing. Enjoy.

NATIVE AMERICAN MOON CALENDAR

THE NATIVE AMERICANS of North America lived surrounded by nature. They hunted and gathered the riches of the earth and honored the animals and plants that were so important to their survival. Native Americans kept track of the passing of time and the months of the year by watching the moon. In this activity, you too will track the passing of time by making a small calendar with the different moons. The names in this calendar were used by Native Americans in the northern and eastern parts of the United States.

Native Americans developed a written language with which to communicate. They used symbols called pictographs on pottery, in silverwork and leatherwork, in weavings and in sand paintings. These symbols included all things in nature such as the sun, the moon, rain, snow, clouds, mountains, and animals.

WHAT YOU WILL NEED

- *12 sheets of 8 1/2 x 11 paper*
- *pencil*
- *tracing paper*
- *black fine line marker*
- *colored pencils, colored markers*
- *current calendar*
- *stapler*

HOW TO DO IT

1. *Each sheet of paper is for one calendar month. Begin by writing the name of the month at the top of the sheet of paper in one color. Then underneath it write the Native American name for the month in another color. Following a current calendar as a guide, use half of the sheet of paper to draw out the days and weeks of the month.*

2. *Now decorate the rest of the calendar page using Native American designs and symbols. Follow the directions on page 7 to copy the designs that you have chosen. Copy the symbols free hand using a pencil first to sketch them in. Go over the pencil lines with black fine marker and then color in as you wish. Do this for each calendar page.*

3. *After you have finished your calendar, staple it at the top with one staple in the center and another one on each side of it close to the edge of the paper.*

13

January—"Full Wolf Moon"—During this cold, dark time, wolves were likely to attack villages when they were not able to find food elsewhere.

February—"Full Snow Moon"—The heaviest snows of the year fell during this month and prevented good hunting. February was also called the "Full Hunger Moon."

March—"Full Worm Moon"—Spring officially began when the ground softened up. Worms returned to the surface and this brought back the robins who fed on them, a sign of the spring season to come.

April—"Full Pink Moon"—The name told what was happening in nature. Wild ground phlox, one of the earliest flowers of spring, spread its brightness in a carpet of pink in the fields.

May—"Full Flower Moon"—Named because of the many colorful flowers that bloomed in May. During this month the animals began to eat the fresh spring grass and produce more milk for their young.

June—"Full Strawberry Moon"—The Algonkian-speaking Native Americans called June the "Full Strawberry Moon." The sweet strawberries of early summer appeared. Baby animals enjoy the warm days.

July—"Full Buck Moon"—During this time, the buck deer's antlers grow. Another common name for July was "Full Thunder Moon," because of the many thunderstorms during the month.

August—"Full Sturgeon Moon"—The "Full Sturgeon Moon" and the "Green Corn Moon" both describe August as it was known to the Native Americans.

September—"Harvest Moon"—At this time of year, the moon was shining brightly above the horizon, allowing workers in the fields to continue gathering the ripe crops late into the evening.

October—"Full Hunter's Moon"—The animals were fat from summer grazing, and with winter coming, it was time to hunt. Also known as "Indian Summer," a warm time that was appreciated before winter's blasts.

November—"Full Beaver Moon"—A time when the beaver traps were set so that the supply of winter furs could be replenished.

December—"Full Cold Month"—This time of year brought very long and cold nights. Storytelling filled the hours.

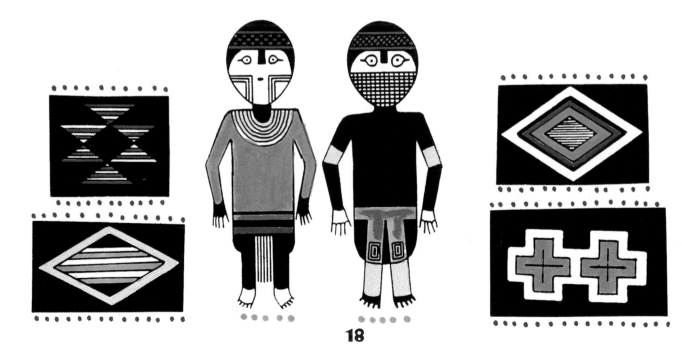

HOPI CORN DANCE

IMAGINE AN EAR OF CORN — sweet, crisp, and delicious. For the Hopi, Native Americans who live in the Southwest, corn or maize as they call it, is a symbol of life. Almost all Hopi religious ceremonies center around the growing of corn. Since their land has little rain, the Hopi, who live mainly in pueblos, or adobe dwellings, ask for help from nature.

In spring, summer, and early autumn, the Hopi hold feasts and dances to give thanks for the planting season and the harvest. These dances are their way of getting closer to nature.

The Corn Dance, as with all Southwestern ceremonies, is a combination of song, drama, dance, and poetry. It is time for prayers for rain, harvests, animals and plants, and the well-being of the pueblo. Dancers dress in elaborate, traditional costumes and headdresses. They begin their steps inside the kiva, or ceremonial room of the pueblo. Then they climb out of the kiva opening like spirits who bring a message to the people. Imagine how the costumes catch the light as the dancers twirl in time to the music.

HOPI CORN DANCE DOLLS

In this activity, you are going to create figures wearing typical Corn Dance outfits. One figure is a girl named Moon Beam and the other is a boy named Rain Cloud. Both are Corn Dance Dolls. Each is wearing a typical corn dance outfit. The boy is holding a drum and wearing a woven blanket around his waist. The girl is also wearing a woven band around her waist. Both have silver and turquoise jewelry on. There is also a Hopi olla, or jar, that the girl might carry on her head and a Hopi kachina doll.

WHAT YOU WILL NEED

- *white oak tag*
- *pencil*
- *tracing paper*
- *black fine line marker*
- *colored pencils or markers*
- *scissors*

HOW TO DO IT

1. *Follow the directions on page 7 and copy the designs on to the white oak tag. Go over the pencil lines with the black fine line marker. Color in the dancers and then carefully cut them out.*

FRENCH CANADIAN THANKSGIVING

WHAT COMES TO MIND when you think of Thanksgiving? Family? Turkey? Autumn leaves? Throughout Canada, on the second Monday in October, people celebrate Thanksgiving Day. The first Thanksgiving for all the Canadian provinces was October 9, 1879. Canadian Thanksgiving Day is similar to the one celebrated in the United States. There is a huge feast that includes turkey, seasonal vegetables, breads, fruits, and special desserts.

In the French-speaking province of Quebec, families and communities gather together on Thanksgiving Day to celebrate the gifts of the land. At this time of year in Canada, the days grow shorter and the harvest moon is in the sky. Maple trees show off their vivid fall colors and delicious apples for eating and cooking are ready to be picked. Since Quebec enjoys a French heritage, French foods are added to the traditional holiday dinner. French apple tart and French bread are included as special homemade treats for the holiday table.

BAKE AN APPLE CAKE

How about trying your hand at making a juicy apple cake? You don't have to wait for Thanksgiving. You'll be thankful you made this simple and delicious apple recipe any time of the year!

INGREDIENTS

- 1 1/2 cups corn oil
- 2 cups sugar
- 3 eggs
- 3 cups all-purpose flour
- 1 teaspoon cinnamon
- 1 teaspoon baking soda
- 1 teaspoon vanilla
- 3 cups apples, peeled, cored and thickly sliced
- extra corn oil to grease the tube pan
- confectioner's sugar

WHAT YOU WILL NEED

- large mixing bowl
- mixing spoon
- measuring cups and spoons
- 9 inch tube pan
- pot holders
- toothpick
- sifter

HOW TO DO IT

1. Ask an adult to help you with the cooking. Preheat the oven to 350 degrees. In the large mixing bowl, stir the oil and sugar together. Add the eggs and beat until the mixture is creamy.
2. Add the flour, cinnamon, baking soda, and vanilla. Stir until completely combined.
3. Add the apples to the batter and stir well.
4. With the extra corn oil, grease the tube pan well. Put the batter into the tube pan. Bake for one hour and 15 minutes. Insert a toothpick into the cake and if it comes out clean the cake is done. It should be a lovely golden brown on top. Allow the cake to cool in the pan before turning it out. Sift some confectioner's sugar on top and serve warm. Makes 10-12 servings.

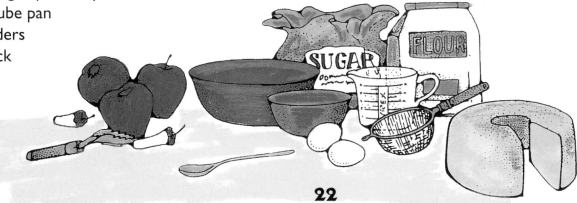

INCA FESTIVAL OF AYMURRAY

THE INCAS WERE AN ancient South American people who lived from about the 1000s to the 1500s. They had a large empire in the Andes Mountains. The center of the Inca empire was in Cuzco, in what is now Peru. Inca society was based on agriculture and its religion centered on sun worship. The people believed that their king was descended from the sun. They felt that he represented the sun on the earth.

Most of the Incas were farmers and for them there was no separation between daily life and religion. Growing food was a religious act. They believed that life was controlled by the powers that were present in the mountains, rivers, lakes, and even in the stones at the edge of a planted field. The growing of corn, or maize, was considered holy. The Incas worked together in the fields planting the kernels of corn and praying to the gods for a good harvest.

Today, high up in the Andes Mountains, live the Quechuas. These people are descendants of the ancient Incas. They celebrate the harvest with a festival called Aymurray. The Quechuas have combined ancient practices with Christianity. For them, the festival is a time of great celebration and happiness. Brightly-colored ornaments and flowers decorate the countryside and music from flutes and guitars can be heard for many miles.

MAKE A SUN T-SHIRT

The sun is as important to us as it was to the ancient Incas. We need it to grow food, as well as to get energy and light. In this activity, you will create your own sun T-shirt. How will you represent the sun?

WHAT YOU WILL NEED

- *white cotton T-shirt*
- *pencil*
- *tracing paper*
- *newspaper*
- *cardboard*
- *tape*
- *fine line black fabric marker*
- *fabric paint markers in yellow, orange, red, and gold*

HOW TO DO IT

1. *Follow the directions on page 7 and copy the sun design on page 25 on to the tracing paper.*

2. *Place some newspaper on to your working surface. Lay the T-shirt with the front facing you on top of the newspaper.*

3. *Cut the cardboard down so that it fits between the front and back of the T-shirt. You will need this so that you have a flat surface on which to draw and paint your sun design and also to keep the paint markers from seeping through the front of the shirt onto the back.*

4. *Slip the cardboard into place and then flatten out the T-shirt.*

5. *Center the tracing paper with the design on it over the T-shirt (the side of the tracing paper that you rubbed your pencil on should be facing down on the T-shirt).*

6. *Draw over the original pencil lines, pressing hard. Now remove the tape and tracing paper and go over the lines with the black fine line fabric marker.*

7. *Using the other fabric marker color in the sun. Make the rays with the gold marker and put some details like dots around the sun in gold.*

8. *Allow the markers to "set" for about an hour. Place a sheet over the finished sun and ask an adult to iron over the design according to the marker's instructions. This will keep the colors permanent.*

SUGAR CANE FESTIVAL IN BARBADOS

SUGAR— WHAT WOULD life be like without it? What would our cakes and candy and even medicines taste like? The introduction of sugar cane and the sugar that was taken from the plant changed the food that we eat. From ancient times until the Middle Ages honey had been the only available sweetener. Sugar cane was introduced to Europe in the Middle Ages. It was called the "Indian honey-bearing reed." But it was very expensive. Later, sugar-cane plants were introduced by Spanish and Portuguese explorers of the 1400s and 1500s.

Barbados, an island in the West Indies, was probably discovered by the Portuguese. The first European settlement was made by the English in 1627. Barbados has the perfect conditions for producing sugar cane — rich soil and a moderate climate. While sugar cane is the island's major product, molasses, rum, coconuts, bananas, and fishing are also part of the island's economy.

In Barbados, the sugar cane is harvested in late May and early June. A harvest festival, called Crop Over, is usually held at the end of July or the beginning of August. It is a time of music, joy, and celebration.
The sugar cane is harvested by cutting down the plant stalks, which are then pressed several times to remove the juice. When the juice evaporates, a dark, sticky sugar is left. This sugar is often sold locally. After the plants are harvested, a feast is prepared and shared with family and friends.

BARBADOS QUICK BREAD

In addition to producing sugar cane, Barbados is also known for a delicious quick bread that is made from bananas, coconut, and honey. While some say it is called quick bread because of how simple it is to make, after you taste it, you may say that it was given its name because of how quickly it disappears!

INGREDIENTS

- *1/3 cup sweet butter*
- *1/3 cup honey*
- *1/3 cup sugar*
- *1 3/4 cup all-purpose flour*
- *2 teaspoons baking powder*
- *1/2 teaspoon salt*
- *1 egg*
- *2 bananas, peeled and mashed*
- *1/2 cup shredded coconut flakes*
- *vegetable oil to grease the pan*

WHAT YOU WILL NEED

- *large mixing bowl*
- *mixing spoon*
- *measuring cups and spoons*
- *9 in. x 5 in. loaf pan*
- *pot holders*
- *toothpick*

HOW TO DO IT

1. *Ask an adult to help you with the cooking. Preheat the oven to 350 degrees.*
2. *In the large mixing bowl combine butter, honey, and sugar. Stir until creamy.*
3. *Add the flour, baking powder, and salt. Combine well.*
4. *Add the egg, mashed bananas, and coconut. Combine completely.*
5. *Grease the loaf pan with the vegetable oil. Pour the batter in the pan. Bake the bread for about an hour or until a toothpick inserted into the center of it comes out clean. The top should be brown and it will smell delicious. Allow the bread to cool before slicing. Makes about 8-10 slices*

SWISS ONION FESTIVAL

ACROSS THE FARMING regions of Europe, festivals are held at harvest time. After the crops have been brought in, and the hard work is done, it is time to celebrate. Some of the harvest festivals in Europe are also special market days. One especially colorful market day takes place in the Swiss city of Bern.

This holiday started in 1405. In that year, Bern was almost destroyed by a huge fire. One hundred volunteers from the neighboring town of Fribourg came to the rescue and helped rebuild the city of Bern. The people of Bern were so grateful that they allowed the people of Fribourg to sell their farm products at the Bern market. The only important farm product that Fribourg had was onions. Ever since that time, an onion market is held in the Bern market square.

On the day of the Bern onion market, the square is filled with onions. They are piled high in wagons, boxes, and baskets. Other farm products are displayed, too. People come from far away to celebrate and to buy the flavorful onions. Local cooks serve onion soup, onion stuffed sausages, onion salad, and even onion tart. Children buy candy in the shape of onions. People have a great time as they celebrate the abundance of the harvest.

SWISS ONION SOUP

Swiss onion soup makes a hearty wintertime meal. Besides having onions in it, this soup is full of many kinds of harvest vegetables. You could serve it in a big steaming bowl with slices of fresh-baked bread. An apple cake would be a perfect dessert.

INGREDIENTS

- 4 medium, yellow onions, peeled and diced
- 4 carrots, peeled and sliced
- 4 potatoes, peeled and sliced
- 1 ear yellow corn, peeled and with kernels removed
- 1/2 cup dried celery
- 1 8 oz. can of peeled and crushed tomatoes with their liquid
- 1/2 cup green zucchini, sliced up
- 1 cup green beans, trimmed and cut in half
- 2 tablespoons sweet butter
- 2 cups vegetable broth
- 4 cups water
- 1 tablespoon salt
- 1 teaspoon oregano
- parmesan cheese, grated

WHAT YOU WILL NEED

- 1 large pot with a lid
- mixing spoon
- measuring cups and spoons

HOW TO DO IT

1. Ask an adult to help you do the cooking. Combine everything in the large pot and bring the soup to a boil, over medium high heat. Cook this way for about 20 minutes.

2. After the soup has boiled, put the lid on the pot. Turn down the heat to low and cook the soup for about 30 more minutes.

3. Serve the soup warm with some grated cheese on top. Use about a tablespoon for each serving. Serves 6. Store the leftover soup in the refrigerator.

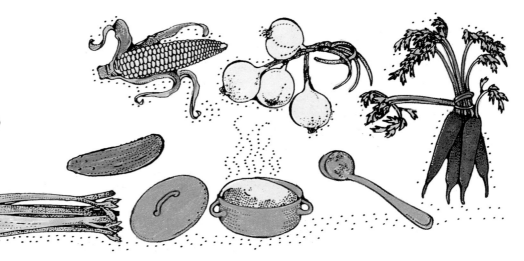

ENGLISH HARVEST HOME

Have you ever seen little corn dolls or ornaments on front doors during the autumn months? The custom of making and displaying corn dolls began in ancient England. This traditional English harvest ritual is part of the festival called Harvest Home or Ingathering. It is still celebrated in rural parts of the British Isles.

People in the countryside celebrate the last harvest by singing, dancing, and decorating the village with branches of dried flowers, fruits, and vegetables that have just been harvested. During the festival, they take the last sheaf of corn, called the cailleac, and form it into a doll. This doll represents the spirit of the field. The harvesters soak the doll with water as a rain charm, or form of good luck. This sheaf is then saved until the spring planting.

MAKE A CORN HUSK DOLL

In this activity, you will make a corn doll to celebrate the ancient English harvest. There are two versions of the doll—a girl and a boy. Since each husk doll is unique, you will have a chance to make your doll with your own personal touch. You can use an old piece of clothing to make the outfit, a button that you have saved, an old coin, lucky piece, special lace or piece of scrap paper. Anything that you choose to attach to your doll will make it special!

WHAT YOU WILL NEED

The supplies are basically the same for each doll:
- *2 ears of corn are needed to make 1 doll*
- *4 cotton balls or crumpled up tissues*
- *black fine line marker*
- *scraps of yarn or string for hair*
- *string to tie doll together*
- *scissors, paper towels, glue, heavy book*
- *scraps of fabric, felt, or worn out clothes*
- *anything that is special to you—lace, small beads, buttons, postage stamps—to decorate your doll*

HOW TO DO IT

1. *Peel the husks off of each ear of corn. Place the husks on some paper towels and cover with a heavy book. Allow them to air dry for a day or so. Try to keep the pieces whole and as long as possible. After they are dry you can proceed with the rest of the directions.*

2. *Make the doll's head. Take the cotton balls or tissue and form it into a large ball the size of a walnut. Place two husks down on your working surface and then put the cotton balls or tissue on top of it. This forms the back of the doll. Place two more husks on top of the cotton and glue the husks together at the top to make the head. Allow this to dry.*

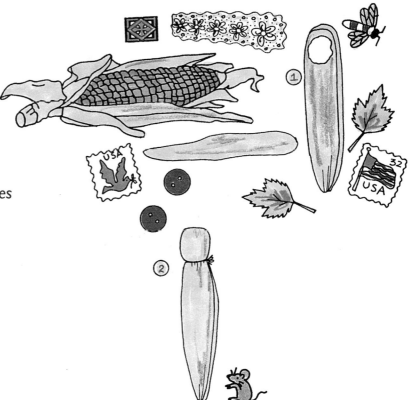

31

3. To make the neck, tie a piece of string underneath the head.

4. Slip two more corn husks underneath the neck to form the arms. Tie a string around the waist of the doll and at the end of the arms to form hands.

5. Divide the husks in half to make legs and tie with string to make feet.

6. Decide whether your doll will be a girl or boy. Use small scraps of fabric to cut out pants, a skirt, and scarves. Glue and tie them on to the doll.

7. With the black marker draw a face and then make hair out of string or yarn and glue in place. Now you can personalize your doll with your collected treasures.

EGYPTIAN FESTIVAL IN HONOR OF MIN

EVERY YEAR THE Nile River in ancient Egypt would flood. This flood gave Egypt its fertile, or rich farming land. The flood waters would spread over the Nile River Valley in the summer. By October the ground was covered with a thick layer of black silt. Farmers were now ready to plow and sow such crops as barley, flax, and wheat. Barley was harvested to make bread and beer. This was the main diet of the people. Flax was woven into linen clothes. Today the Nile still provides for the people of Egypt as they tend the soil and harvest the crops like their ancestors.

The ancient Egyptians did not have holidays like we have today. Instead, they had many festivals and holy days throughout the year. One of the most important festivals was a harvest festival in honor of Min, the god Egyptians believed made the earth fertile. The festival of Min lasted several days. There was music, dancing, acrobats, jugglers, and feasting. As part of the celebration, people carried images of Min through the streets.

DRAW AN ANCIENT EGYPTIAN HARVEST SCENE

What would it have been like to be part of the festival of Min? In this activity, you will step back in time to ancient Egypt and draw a scene of the harvest. You will also create some hieroglyphs—a Greek word meaning "sacred writing in stone," and include them in the activity.

WHAT YOU WILL NEED

- white oak tag, 10 in. x 20 in. (2 pieces are needed, one one for the harvest festival scene and one to write the hieroglyphs).
- pencil
- tracing paper
- tape
- black fine line marker
- colored markers or pencils

HOW TO DO IT

1. To make the harvest festival scene follow the directions given on page 7 to transfer the design on to the oak tag. Now take the design that's on the tracing paper and center it on the oak tag. Tape it down gently and then go over the design with your pencil. (The rubbed side should face the oak tag.) Go over the pencil line with black fine line marker and then color in.

2. To make the hieroglyphs you can just draw them freehand onto the oak tag and then color them in as you like. If you like, you can draw them first in pencil and then go over them with the black fine line marker. Have fun studying and exploring their meaning.

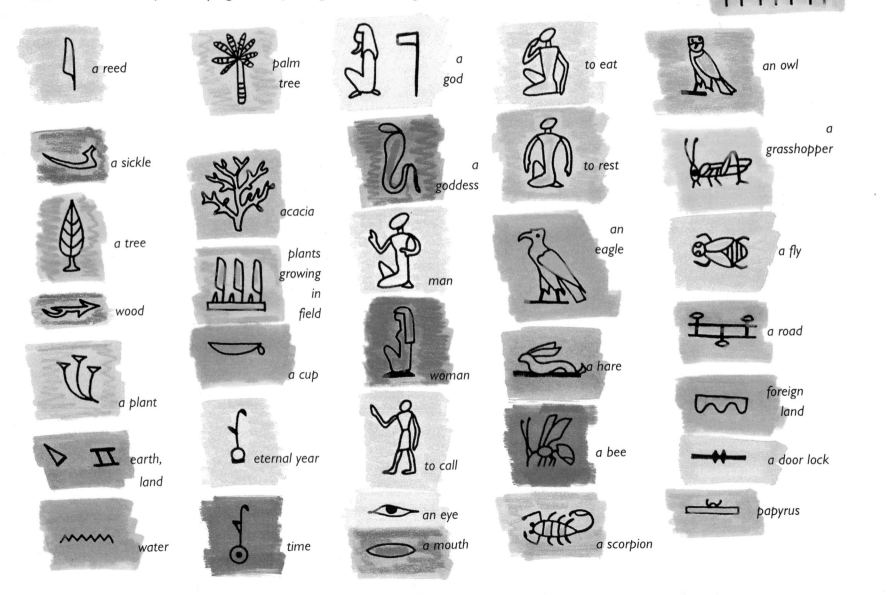

a reed

a sickle

a tree

wood

a plant

earth, land

water

palm tree

acacia

plants growing in field

a cup

eternal year

time

a god

a goddess

man

woman

to call

an eye

a mouth

to eat

to rest

an eagle

a hare

a bee

a scorpion

an owl

a grasshopper

a fly

a road

foreign land

a door lock

papyrus

ISRAEL—THE FESTIVAL OF THE BOOTHS

IN SEPTEMBER OR October it is common to see blue and gold booths scattered throughout many Jewish neighborhoods. These booths, or succahs, celebrate the eight-day long holiday Succoth. This ancient festival, which began in biblical times, originally celebrated the harvest of grapes and olives, two important crops in the Middle East. At harvest time, farmers lived in booths in the fields so that they could keep an eye on their crops.

Today Succoth is celebrated by Jewish people around the world. Succahs are built in open spaces — gardens, roofs, porches, courtyards, and parks. The roof of a succah is made of olive and other tree branches, and the sides are a blue and gold cloth. Young people decorate the inside of a succah with seasonal fruits and vegetables —all symbols of plenty. Corn, wheat, apples, dried flowers, pumpkins, onions, grapes, apricots, squash, dates, figs, pomegranates, almost any fruit or vegetable is tied to the branches of the succah. Spaces are left between the branches and the fruits and vegetables so that the stars can be seen and the rain can come in. This is to remind people that they must look to heaven for protection.

Family and friends gather inside the succah for meals during the festival. Some people even sleep in the succah, as their ancestors did years before. A special ceremony is held every day. Palm leaves are bound together with myrtle and willow twigs. This is called a lulav and held in one hand. A lemon-like fruit, called an etrog, is held in the other hand. Both hands are joined together, a blessing is said, and the hands are pointed in six directions — east, south, north, west, up, and down. This shows that God is everywhere.

BUILD A MINIATURE SUCCAH

IN THIS ACTIVITY, you will make a miniature succah. All you need is a shoe box, clay, and paint. Think about how you will decorate your succah. Which seasonal fruits and vegetables will you include? If you decide to include an etrog and a lulav, you may want to find out the traditional blessing that is said over them.

WHAT YOU WILL NEED

- shoebox
- scissors
- glue
- colored markers
- acrylic paints
- paint brushes
- cardboard base for succah
- 1 cup flour
- 1/2 cup salt
- 1/4 cup water
- 1 tablespoon vegetable oil
- mixing bowl
- spoon
- cookie sheet covered with aluminum foil
- clear nail polish

HOW TO DO IT

1. *A succah is made up of a roof and four posts. Cut the shoe box so that the bottom of it forms the roof and it has 4 posts to hold up the roof. Glue the cardboard base. Draw some vines and leaves along the posts and roof with the colored markers.*

2. *In the mixing bowl combine the flour, salt, and water. Mix well. Form the homemade clay into miniature fruits and vegetables. Place them on the cookie sheet. Ask an adult to help you with the cooking. Place the cookie sheet in a 250 degree oven for 5-10 minutes. Watch them carefully so they don't burn.*

3. *Allow the clay to cool and then paint with the acrylic colors. If you like you can coat them with clear nail polish. Glue them on to the succah's roof and posts. Arange some inside the succah and glue on to the base.*

NIGERIAN HARVEST MASKS

IN AFRICA, HARVEST festivals are part of everyday life. People celebrate the harvest with art, music, and song. Everyone participates in the songs — either singing or playing an instrument. Musicians often play the agogo and other instruments made of wood, iron, skin, and hollow logs.

In Nigeria, a country in western Africa, masked dancers and musicians come from Asaba along the Niger River. Their dance is performed at an important time of the growing season. Their masks tell about the farming activities of the Ekpo people. Artists paint designs on the masks to show life in the village and along the river. The turtle is a favorite image and so are the lizard, sun, moon, and trees. All of these have special meanings to the people. The turtle means long life. Pictures of turtles show a shell divided into sections, one for each month of the year.

THE NIGERIAN HARVEST mask is full of meaning. On each side is a turtle design which symbolizes a good harvest and a long life. Follow the directions on page 7 and transfer the design on to the oak tag or cardboard. Draw over the pencil lines with a black marker so that the patterns show up. Cut it out. Make two small holes at each side by the ears and two small holes in the eyes. Tie a piece of string through the ear holes. Now you can wear the mask.

WHAT YOU WILL NEED

- *tan oak tag or cardboard*
- *pencil*
- *tracing paper*
- *black marker*
- *scissors*
- *string*

YAM FESTIVAL IN GHANA

THE YAM FESTIVAL in Ghana, a country in western Africa, is called the "To Hoot at Famine." This festival is held once a year in the beginning of August, just as the rainy season is coming to an end. At this time, the crops are ripe and ready for harvest. There is plenty of dry corn, or maize, as well as other vegetables such as okra, beans, and yams. Yams are the first fruits of the harvest. The yam is the main food of the people in western Africa. It is a large tuberous root related to the sweet potato. Yams can be cooked or dried and pounded into flour. Since a good yam harvest is important for survival, all of the people give thanks to the spirits of the earth and sky.

Women dig up the yams and carry them home in baskets on their heads. Everyone is proud of the harvest and wants to be the family with the largest crop. People gather together as the women and young girls prepare the feast. The yams are the prized food. A young boy is chosen to carry the best yams and he is followed to the festival dinner by another boy beating a drum. Other young people from the village march to the beat of the drum and the sound of a woodwind instrument. Chiefs, beneath their umbrellas, follow the yams, and the young people dance. Everyone enjoys the feast and is thankful and happy for the good harvest.

MAKE YAM MUFFINS

Have you ever eaten a yam? How was it prepared? In this activity, you'll make yam muffins. Maybe you'll want to share them with a family member and include them in a special family meal.

INGREDIENTS

- 1 cup canned yams, mashed
- 1 3/4 cups all-purpose flour
- 1/2 teaspoon salt
- 1/2 cup sugar
- 2 teaspoons baking powder
- 2 eggs
- 4 tablespoons of sweet butter, melted
- 3/4 cup milk
- 1 teaspoon cinnamon

WHAT YOU WILL NEED

- large mixing bowl
- mixing spoon
- measuring cups and spoons
- muffin tins and paper muffin cups
- pot holder

HOW TO DO IT

1. Ask an adult to help you with the cooking. Preheat the oven to 350 degrees.
2. In the large mixing bowl combine all of the ingredients and mix well.
3. Pour the batter into the prepared muffin tins two-thirds full and bake for 20-25 minutes. Makes 24 muffins.

HOUNEN-ODORI IN JAPAN

IF SOMEONE ASKS you to go to a Hounen-Odori, where would the person be inviting you? Why, to a harvest festival in Japan. Harvest festivals in Japan, like those around the world, are a time of celebration. The harvest festival takes place on the fifteenth day of the harvest moon in the month of August. This is a time when the moon shines brightly and lights the way for the people as they harvest the crops. The harvest is celebrated mainly in villages and rural districts and takes many different forms.

Traveling through the beautiful Japanese countryside during Hounen-Odori, you might see different celebrations in every community that you visit. In some areas, large platforms are built in the village center. In others, a newly harvested field will be chosen as a place to dance. Fruits of the harvest, including garlands of flowers, both real and artificial, add to the festive spirit.

Musicians come from all over Japan to play in the villages. They often dress in a traditional kimono. Feasting is part of every harvest celebration, and women from each family prepare delicious foods to be eaten by the light of the full harvest moon.

JAPANESE FOLDED FLOWERS

JAPAN IS FAMOUS for its ancient craft of paper folding called origami. One piece of paper is folded to create intereting objects. In this activity, you will make beautiful flowers in vivid colors, like the ones that grow in the Japanese countryside.

WHAT YOU WILL NEED

- *8 in. square of colored paper, one for each flower*
- *8 straws for the flower's stem*
- *1 sheet of green paper for the leaves*
- *pencil*
- *ruler*
- *scissors*
- *stapler*
- *white glue*

HOW TO DO IT

1. *Measure and mark an inch along one side of the sheet of colored paper. Draw a line connecting the marks. You will use this line to make your first fold on.*

2. *Fold the paper along the pencilled line and then make seven other folds like a fan. Fold the "fan" in half to form the flower. Staple the flower to the straw.*

3. *Cut out two leaves from the green paper and glue in place.*

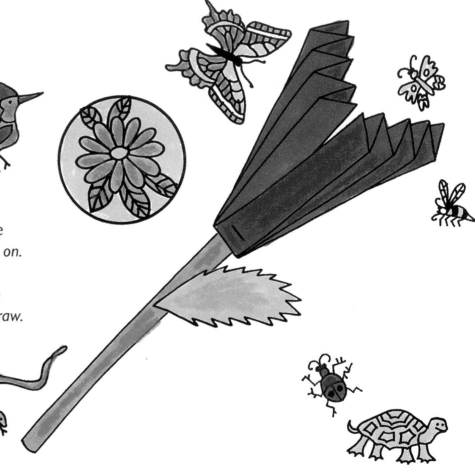

BIRTHDAY OF THE MOON IN CHINA

THE MOON IS VERY important to the people of China. They calculate the passage of time by watching the phases of the moon. Farmers plant and harvest according to the cycles of the moon. The moon means so much to the people of China that they even celebrate its birthday with a festival.

The Birthday of the Moon festival occurs in mid-Autumn, on the fifteenth day of the eighth month, around the end of September. There are thirteen months in a Chinese year because they use a lunar calendar.

During the moon festival, people eat traditional small, round cakes called mooncakes. These cakes are also called the circle of happiness. The cakes are made of a grayish flour and are often filled with nuts, spices, and sugar. Today you can buy these mooncakes in pastry shops. Many women also make them to give as gifts. They hope that this will bring about a good future and a good harvest.

The Chinese had a legend that the hare lived in the moon. In ancient times, Chinese women built an altar in the courtyard of their house. A figure of a long-eared hare was in the center of the altar. In front of the hare was a dish with thirteen mooncakes, one for each new moon of the year.

MAKE CHINESE MOONCAKES

WOULD YOU LIKE to celebrate the moon's birthday? In this activity, you will make little mooncakes as part of the celebration. Maybe you would like to bake an extra batch to give as a gift to a friend.

These little mooncakes are shaped into small balls. These balls represent the moon and the circle of happiness. You can poke your thumb gently through the center of each mooncake and place a tiny bit of jam to sweeten the harvest and bring good luck.

INGREDIENTS

- *1/2 cup salted butter*
- *1/4 cup sugar*
- *1 egg yolk*
- *1 cup all-purpose flour, heaping*
- *jam (about 1 cup)*

WHAT YOU WILL NEED

- *large mixing bowl*
- *mixing spoon*
- *measuring cups and spoons*
- *aluminum foil*
- *cookie sheets*
- *pot holders*

HOW TO DO IT

1. *Ask an adult to help you with the cooking. In the large mixing bowl, combine the butter, sugar, and egg yolk. Stir until creamy and combine completely.*
2. *Add the flour and mix thoroughly. Form the dough into one large ball and wrap it in aluminum foil. Put this in the refrigerator for 30 minutes.*
3. *Unwrap the chilled dough and, with clean hands, form small balls in the palms of your hand. These are the mooncakes.*
4. *Make a hole with your thumb gently in the center of each mooncake and fill with about half a teaspoon of your favorite jam.*
5. *Preheat the oven to 375 degrees. Cover the cookie sheets with aluminum foil. Bake the mooncakes for about 20 minutes or just until the outside edges are slightly brown. Makes about 24 mooncakes.*

RICE HARVEST FESTIVAL IN INDIA

SINCE MOST OF the states of India have their own languages, the holiday of the rice festival has many different names. In all of the states in the south, though, people make a special sweet, or treat, of rice, sugar, fruits, and butter to celebrate the harvest. In the state of Tamilnad, this sweet is called pongal. That is also the name of their rice festival.

Pongal lasts for three days. For many days before, however, everyone is busy preparing for the festival. Young people coat the walls of the village homes with fresh whitewash or fresh red clay to cover the streaks from last season's rain. They may also paint designs on the walls or draw them on the floors with colored rice powder.

On the first day of Pongal, people thank the gods for sending rain to make a good harvest. On the second day, thanks are given to the sun. The third day of the holiday honors the cattle who have helped to plow the fields and to gather the harvest. Men and boys take the family water buffalo to a watering hole to wash it. Then they paint the animal's horns a bright color — maybe gold or blue. Sometimes they add blue-green peacock feathers. Girls may hang garlands of flowers around the necks of the hardworking beasts.

MAKE A TREAT FOR PONGAL AND A WATER BUFFALO

How would you like to prepare a sweet for Pongal? In this activity, you'll be able to make such a treat as well as mold a small water buffalo out of homemade clay.

SWEET TREAT

Yogurt is often served as part of an Indian meal. Here is a sweet treat made with yogurt that is a fun dessert. You can top it with semi-sweet chocolate pieces, cherries, or a sprinkling of cinnamon and sugar.

INGREDIENTS

- *2 8 oz. containers of vanilla yogurt*
- *1/4 cup granola*
- *1/4 cup raisins*
- *1/4 cup shredded coconut flakes*
- *6 cherries or 1/4 cup semi-sweet chocolate*
- *pieces or 1/2 teaspoon cinnamon mixed with 3 tablespoons sugar*

WHAT YOU WILL NEED

- *large mixing bowl*
- *mixing spoon*
- *measuring cups and spoons*
- *6 paper muffin cups*

HOW TO DO IT

1. *In the large mixing bowl, combine the yogurt, granola, raisins, and coconut flakes. Mix well.*
2. *Fill each muffin cup half full and cover with your choice of topping. Makes six servings.*

THE WATER BUFFALO
WHAT YOU WILL NEED

- *homemade clay (see page 38 for instructions on how to make this)*
- *cookie sheet*
- *acrylic paints in tan, red, yellow, blue and green*
- *paint brushes*
- *1 in. x 2 in. scrap of fabric (for feed sack)*
- *2 tablespoons of rice (to put in feed sack)*
- *glue*

HOW TO DO IT

1. *Prepare some homemade clay. Starting with a ball about the size of a tennis ball, form the clay into a simple animal shape with a head, legs, tail, and round body. Add pieces of clay for horns. Then place the water buffalo on a cookie sheet and bake at 250 degrees for 5-10 minutes. Ask an adult to help with the baking.*
2. *After the water buffalo has cooled, paint him tan. Then paint some flowers and designs on his back and around his neck. Fold the scrap of fabric in half and glue along the two outside edges to make a little feed sack. Fill it with rice and place it in front of the water buffalo.*